I0465400

The Financial Foundations Series

The Investor's Financial Glossary

Disclaimer:

This book is for educational purposes only. It does not constitute financial advice. Consult a professional before making investment decisions.

Introduction

Welcome to *The Investor's Financial Glossary*.

This dictionary is designed to help you understand key financial terms, whether you're just starting out or looking to refine your knowledge.

With the stock market and investing world full of jargon, this book will simplify complex terms and make them more accessible.

Why I Created This Dictionary

I created this dictionary because I saw the need for a clear and easy-to-understand resource for anyone interested in investing.

Over the years, I've noticed how confusing financial terminology can be, especially for beginners. With my background in writing other stock market books, I wanted to create a tool that demystifies these terms and helps both new and more experienced investors feel more confident in their financial decisions.

How It Can
Benefit All Levels

This glossary is designed to benefit everyone, from beginners to seasoned investors.

Beginners will find simple, easy-to-understand definitions that build their financial vocabulary, while experienced investors can use it to quickly refresh their knowledge or clarify more advanced concepts.

Whether you're investing in stocks, bonds, or other financial instruments, this book helps bridge the gap between jargon and practical understanding.

How It Can Benefit
All Levels

Inside this dictionary, you'll find a wide range of definitions covering everything from basic financial terms to more advanced concepts.

Each entry is designed to be concise and clear, with real-world applications to help connect the term to your investment journey.

You'll also find relevant terms tied to the latest financial trends and tools, such as trading apps, financial news, and market analysis.

How to Make the Most Out of This Book

1. Read Through the Glossary

Start by reading through the glossary from start to finish to familiarize yourself with the terms. Even if you're an experienced investor, you might come across concepts you haven't encountered before.

2. Use It as a Reference Guide

Keep the book handy as a quick reference tool. Whenever you come across an unfamiliar term in financial articles, trading apps, or during your own investing journey, look it up here for a clear and simple explanation.

3. Apply What You Learn

Understanding financial terms is one thing; applying them is another. Use the definitions to gain a deeper understanding of the markets, and incorporate what you learn into your investment strategies.

4. Review Regularly

Revisit the glossary from time to time, especially when you encounter new financial terms or when you're learning about new investment strategies. Regular review will help reinforce your knowledge and improve your confidence in navigating financial discussions.

5. Check Out Our Other Books

We keep adding more books to our collection, each designed to help you improve your financial knowledge and investment skills. Be sure to check out our other stock market books for a more comprehensive learning experience.

How to Use This Dictionary

1. Browse the Alphabetical List

All terms in this glossary are arranged in alphabetical order, making it quick and easy to find the definition you're looking for. Simply look up any term by its first letter and find a concise explanation.

2. Most Important Terms Are <u>Underlined</u>

The most important and frequently used terms in the world of finance are <u>underlined</u> for easy identification. These terms are essential to understanding the basics of investing and can provide a strong foundation for your financial knowledge.

3. Explore Related Terms

Some terms in the glossary are related to each other. For example, when looking up a specific financial ratio, you may come across other terms that provide additional context or are crucial for understanding. Feel free to jump between terms to build a more comprehensive understanding.

Key Stock Market Concepts

What is the Stock Market?

The stock market is a platform where shares of publicly traded companies are bought and sold. It serves as a marketplace for investors to trade ownership stakes in companies, enabling businesses to raise capital and individuals to invest in future growth. Major stock exchanges, such as the New York Stock Exchange (NYSE) and NASDAQ, facilitate these trades.

Basic Principles of Investing

- Risk and Reward: Investments carry varying levels of risk, and returns are generally proportional to the risk taken. Diversification can help balance this.

- Long-Term Perspective: Successful investing often requires patience and a focus on long-term growth rather than short-term gains.

- Compound Growth: Reinvesting earnings can significantly boost the value of investments over time, thanks to compounding.

Types of Financial Instruments

Equity Instruments

- Stocks
- Preferred Stock
- Warrants

Debt Instruments

- Bonds
- Treasury Bills (T-Bills)
- Corporate Bonds
- Municipal Bonds
- Commercial Paper
- Certificates of Deposit

Derivatives

- Options
- Futures
- Swaps
- Forwards
- Credit Default Swaps (CDS)

Investment Funds

- Mutual Funds
- Exchange-Traded Funds (ETFs)
- Hedge Funds
- Private Equity Funds

Alternative Instruments

- Real Estate Investment Trusts (REITs)
- Commodities
- Cryptocurrencies

"The stock market is a device for transferring money from the impatient to the patient."

– Warren Buffett

"Know what you own, and know why you own it."

– Peter Lynch

- **Accumulation ETF**: ETFs that reinvest dividends.

- **Accumulated Other Comprehensive Income (Loss)**: Unrealized gains or losses not included in net income.

- **Active Management**: An investment approach in which portfolio managers make specific investments to outperform a benchmark index. Opposed to passive management, where the goal is to match an index.

- **Adjusted Closing Price:** The closing price of a security after adjustments for dividends and stock splits, giving a more accurate reflection of the security's value over time.

- **Alpha:** A measure of an investment's performance relative to a benchmark. Positive alpha indicates outperformance, while negative alpha suggests underperformance.

- **American Depositary Receipt (ADR):** A certificate representing shares in a foreign company that trades on a U.S. exchange. ADRs allow U.S. investors to invest in foreign companies more easily.

- **Amortization**: The process of spreading out the cost of an asset or loan over time. Amortization often applies to intangible assets or loans with regular payments.

- **Annual Percentage Rate (APR)**: The annual rate charged for borrowing or earned through an investment, expressed as a percentage. APR includes any fees or additional costs.

- **Annualized Return:** The average return of an investment over a year, standardized to show a yearly performance, even if the investment was held for less than a year.

- **Annuity:** A financial product sold by insurance companies that pays out a fixed stream of payments to individuals, primarily used as a retirement income tool.

- **Arbitrage:** The practice of buying and selling the same asset in different markets to profit from a price difference. Arbitrage often minimizes risk for traders.

- **Ask:** The lowest price a seller is willing to accept for a stock or other security. Usually higher than the bid, creating the bid-ask spread.

- **Asset Allocation**: Dividing investments among asset classes like stocks, bonds, and real estate to manage risk and optimize returns.

- **Asset Classes**: Categories of investments with similar characteristics, such as equities, fixed income, and cash equivalents.

- **Asset Turnover**: Measures a company's efficiency in using assets to generate sales. Higher ratio indicates better asset use.

- **Assets Under Management (AUM)**: The total market value of assets a financial institution or individual manages on behalf of clients, indicating the firm's size and success.

- **At-the-Money (ATM):** A term for options when the strike price is the same as the current price of the underlying asset. ATM options have high time value.

- **Averaging Down:** An investment strategy where an investor buys more of a security as its price falls, reducing the average purchase price.

A
B
C
D
E
F
G
H
I
J
K
L
M
N
O
P
Q
R
S
T
U
V
W
X
Y
Z

B

- **Backtesting**: Testing a trading strategy using historical data to see how it would have performed.

- **Balance Sheet**: A financial statement showing a company's assets, liabilities, and equity.

- **Bankruptcy**: The legal process in which a company is unable to repay its debts and must liquidate or reorganize.

- **Basis Point**: One-hundredth of a percentage point, used to measure changes in interest rates or financial ratios.

- **Bear Market:** A prolonged period of declining stock prices, typically by 20% or more. Investors in a bear market may experience pessimism, and the market often sees decreased liquidity.

- **Benchmark**: A standard or point of reference, such as a market index, used to evaluate the performance of an investment portfolio. Examples include the S&P 500 for U.S. equities or the FTSE 100 for UK stocks.

- **Beta:** A measure of a stock's or portfolio's volatility relative to the overall market. A beta greater than 1 indicates greater volatility, while less than 1 suggests lower risk.

- **Bid**: The highest price a buyer is willing to pay for a security. Bid prices typically appear on market exchanges and are part of the bid-ask spread.

- **Bid-Ask Spread**: The difference between the bid price (what buyers are willing to pay) and the ask price (what sellers are asking). The spread is influenced by the liquidity of the security.

- **Blue-Chip Stocks**: Shares of large, established companies with strong financial performance. These companies are often considered low-risk and stable for investors.

- **Bond:** A debt security in which an investor lends money to an entity (government or corporation) in exchange for periodic interest payments and the return of the principal at maturity.

- **Bond Rating:** An evaluation of the creditworthiness of a bond issued by a corporation or government entity. Ratings range from investment-grade to junk, based on risk.

- **Book Value:** The value of a company's assets minus its liabilities, representing its net worth according to its balance sheet. It is often used to assess the value of a company.

A
B
C
D
E
F
G
H
I
J
K
L
M
N
O
P
Q
R
S
T
U
V
W
X
Y
Z

- **Broker**: A person or firm that facilitates the buying and selling of securities for clients. Brokers earn commissions or fees for their services.

- **Bull Market**: A period in which prices in the market rise significantly, usually by 20% or more, driven by investor optimism and economic growth.

- **Burn Rate**: The rate at which a company spends its capital before reaching profitability.

- **Buyback**: When a company purchases its own shares from the market, reducing the number of outstanding shares, often to boost earnings per share or increase the stock price.

- **Buy Limit Order:** A type of order placed to buy a security at a price equal to or lower than a specified limit. This order ensures that an investor does not overpay for a stock.

C

- **Capitalization:** The total market value of a company's outstanding shares. It is calculated by multiplying the share price by the number of shares. Companies are classified into small-cap, mid-cap, or large-cap categories.

- **Capital Expenditure Coverage Ratio**: Operating cash flow divided by capital expenditures.

- **Capital Gains:** The profit earned from the sale of an asset, such as a stock, that has appreciated in value. Capital gains are taxable depending on the holding period.

- **Capital Gains Tax:** A tax on the profit from the sale of assets, such as stocks or real estate. Short-term capital gains are taxed at a higher rate than long-term ones.

- **Cash Conversion Cycle**: The time it takes for a company to convert investments in inventory and receivables back into cash. A shorter cycle is more efficient.

- **Cash Equivalents**: Short-term investments easily convertible to cash.

- **Cash Flow:** The movement of money into and out of a business, used to measure the company's financial health. Positive cash flow is essential for operations and growth.

- **Cash Flow Coverage Ratio**: Operating cash flow divided by total liabilities, showing debt coverage ability.

- **Cash Flow Statement**: A financial statement that shows the cash generated and used during a specific period. It helps assess a company's ability to generate future cash flows.

- **Cash Flow to Debt Ratio**: Operating cash flow as a percentage of total debt, indicating repayment ability.

- **Collateral**: An asset pledged by a borrower to secure a loan, which can be seized by the lender if the borrower defaults.

- **Common Stock**: A type of equity that represents ownership in a company, granting voting rights and potential dividends. Common stockholders are last in line to claim assets if the company is liquidated.

- **Commodity:** A basic good used in commerce that is interchangeable with other goods of the same type. Commodities include oil, gold, and wheat and are often traded in futures markets.

- **Compound Interest**: Interest calculated on both the initial principal and the accumulated interest from previous periods. This leads to exponential growth over time.

- **Consumer Price Index (CPI)**: A measure of the average change over time in the prices of a basket of goods and services typically purchased by households. It is used to assess inflation.

- **Convertible Bond**: A bond that can be converted into a predetermined number of shares of the issuing company, allowing the bondholder to participate in the company's equity upside.

- **Corporate Bond**: A debt security issued by a company to raise capital. Corporate bonds pay periodic interest and return the principal at maturity.

- **Cost of Capital**: The cost a company incurs to raise capital (through debt or equity) to fund its operations and growth. It reflects the risk to investors and is used to evaluate potential investments.

- **Covenant:** A clause in a loan agreement or bond indenture that outlines specific conditions or restrictions on the borrower or issuer to protect the interests of lenders or investors.

A B C D E F G H I J K L M N O P Q R S T U V W X Y Z

- **Creditworthiness**: A measure of a borrower's ability and reliability to repay debt, based on their credit history and financial status.

- **Credit Default Swap (CDS)**: A derivative used by investors to hedge against the risk of default on a bond or loan. CDSs act as insurance against credit risk.

- **Credit Rating**: A score assigned to an entity (such as a company or government) to assess its creditworthiness and likelihood of repaying its debts. Credit ratings influence borrowing costs and investment decisions.

- **Current Assets**: Assets expected to be converted into cash within a year.

A B C D E F G H I J K L M N O P Q R S T U V W X Y Z

D

- **Data vendor**: A company or service that provides financial data, such as stock prices, news, and analysis.

- **Days of Inventory Outstanding (DIO)**: The average number of days a company holds inventory before selling it. Lower DIO is generally better.

- **Days of Payables Outstanding (DPO)**: The average number of days a company takes to pay its payables. Higher DPO can suggest better supplier management.

- **Days of Sales Outstanding (DSO)**: The average number of days it takes for a company to collect receivables. Lower DSO indicates quicker collection.

- **Debt**: Money borrowed by an individual or organization, typically in the form of bonds or loans, which must be repaid with interest.

- **Debt-to-equity ratio**: A measure of a company's financial leverage, calculated by dividing total debt by shareholders' equity.

- **Debt securities**: Financial instruments issued by corporations or governments as a way of borrowing money, such as bonds or notes.

A B C D E F G H I J K L M N O P Q R S T U V W X Y Z

- **Debt swap**: A financial transaction where one set of debt instruments is exchanged for another, often to improve terms or manage risk.

- **Debtor**: An individual or organization that owes money to another party, typically in the form of a loan or credit.

- **Debt Ratio**: Total debt as a percentage of total assets, indicating leverage.

- **Default**: The failure to meet debt repayment obligations as agreed in a loan or bond contract.

- **Defensive stocks**: Stocks that tend to perform well during economic downturns, such as utilities, healthcare, or consumer staples.

- **Deferred Revenue**: Revenue received but not yet earned.

- **Deferred tax asset**: A financial asset that represents a reduction in future tax payments due to deductible temporary differences.

- **Deferred tax liability**: A liability for taxes that a company owes but does not yet have to pay, often due to differences in accounting methods.

- **Deficit**: The situation where expenses exceed income, often used in reference to government budgets or trade balances.

- **Defined contribution plan**: A retirement plan where contributions are made into an individual account, and the benefits depend on the investment performance.

- **Deflation**: A decrease in the general price level of goods and services, often linked to a reduction in the supply of money or credit.

- **Deflationary spiral**: A situation where deflation causes reduced consumer spending, leading to further deflation and economic decline.

- **Deliverable**: The asset or product that must be delivered to settle a futures contract or other financial agreement.

- **Delivery date**: The date on which an asset must be delivered under the terms of a contract.

- **Delta**: A measure of how much an option's price changes when the price of the underlying asset changes.

- **Demand curve**: A graph showing the relationship between the price of an asset and the quantity demanded by buyers.

- **Demutualization**: The process of converting a mutual company (owned by policyholders) into a publicly traded company (owned by shareholders).

- **Derivative**: A financial instrument whose value is derived from the value of an underlying asset, such as options or futures contracts.

- **Depreciation expense**: The amount of depreciation that is recorded as an expense on a company's income statement during a given period.

- **Deposit account**: An account held at a financial institution that allows deposits and withdrawals, such as savings or checking accounts.

- **Depressed market**: A market characterized by lower than usual demand or activity, often due to economic downturns or negative sentiment.

- **Derivative contract**: A contract between two or more parties whose value depends on the price of an underlying asset.

- **Designated market maker (DMM)**: A member of the New York Stock Exchange who is responsible for maintaining fair and orderly markets in specific securities.

- **Discount bond**: A bond that is sold for less than its face value, often due to lower interest rates or high risk.

- **Discount rate**: The interest rate charged by a central bank to commercial banks for short-term loans or the rate used to calculate present value in discounted cash flow analysis.

- **Discretionary income**: Income remaining after taxes and essential expenses, which can be used for discretionary spending or saving.

- **Distribution ETF**: ETFs that pay out dividends to shareholders.

- **Diversification**: The strategy of spreading investments across various assets or sectors to reduce risk.

- **Dividend**: A portion of a company's earnings distributed to shareholders, typically in the form of cash or additional shares.

- **Dividend Paid and CapEx Coverage Ratio:** Measures how much cash flow covers dividends and capital expenditures.

- **Dividend yield**: The annual dividend payment expressed as a percentage of the stock's current price.

- **Dividend reinvestment plan (DRIP)**: A plan that allows shareholders to reinvest their dividends to purchase more shares of the company.

- **Divestiture**: The process of selling or disposing of a company's assets or subsidiaries to focus on core business operations.

- **Dodd-Frank Act**: A U.S. federal law aimed at reducing systemic risk and protecting consumers in the financial industry, following the 2008 financial crisis.

- **Dollar cost averaging**: An investment strategy where a fixed amount is invested regularly, regardless of market conditions, to spread risk over time.

- **Dow Jones Industrial Average (DJIA)**: A stock market index that tracks 30 of the largest publicly traded companies in the U.S.

- **Downside risk**: The potential loss an investment faces due to unfavorable market movements.

- **DPO (Days Payable Outstanding)**: A metric that measures how long a company takes to pay its suppliers after receiving an invoice.

- **Drag along rights**: Rights that allow a majority shareholder to compel minority shareholders to join in the sale of a company.

- **Drawdown**: The reduction in the value of an investment or portfolio from its peak to its lowest point during a specific period.

- **Due Diligence**: The research and analysis conducted before an investment or acquisition.

- **Duties**: Fees or taxes imposed by governments, often on imports or exports, in international trade.

E

- **Earnings**: The profits a company generates after expenses, taxes, and other costs are subtracted from revenue.

- **Earnings per share (EPS)**: A company's earnings divided by the number of outstanding shares, indicating the profitability of a company on a per-share basis.

- **Earnings announcement**: A report issued by a company detailing its earnings performance over a specified period, typically quarterly or annually.

- **Earnings growth**: The rate at which a company's earnings increase over a period, often expressed as a percentage.

- **Earnings before interest, taxes, depreciation, and amortization (EBITDA)**: A measure of a company's profitability that excludes interest, taxes, depreciation, and amortization expenses.

- **Earnings guidance**: A company's estimate of its future earnings, typically issued before the official earnings report.

- **EBIT**: Earnings before interest and taxes.

- **EBIT per Revenue**: Ratio of EBIT to revenue, showing operational efficiency.

- **EBITDA**: Earnings before interest, taxes, depreciation, and amortization.

- **EBT**: Earnings before tax.

- **EBT per EBIT**: Ratio of earnings before tax to earnings before interest and taxes, reflecting tax effects.

- **Economic moat**: A competitive advantage that allows a company to maintain its market position and protect profits from competitors.

- **Economic indicator**: Data used to gauge the economic health of a country or region, such as GDP, inflation rates, or unemployment figures.

- **Economic growth**: The increase in a country's production of goods and services over time, usually measured by GDP growth.

- **Economic value added (EVA)**: A measure of a company's financial performance that calculates the value created beyond the required return on its capital.

- **Effective interest rate**: The true interest rate after considering the effect of compounding over a period.

A B C D E F G H I J K L M N O P Q R S T U V W X Y Z

- **Effective Tax Rate**: Average tax rate a company pays on its earnings.

- **Efficiency ratio**: A financial ratio used to assess how well a company utilizes its assets and liabilities to generate income.

- **Efficient market hypothesis (EMH)**: The theory that all publicly available information is already reflected in stock prices, making it impossible to consistently outperform the market.

- **Elasticity**: A measure of how much the quantity demanded or supplied of an asset changes in response to price changes.

- **Electronic trading:** The use of computer systems and networks to facilitate the buying and selling of financial securities.

- **Emerging markets:** Economies of developing countries that are becoming more integrated into the global market, often characterized by rapid growth and higher risk.

- **Employee stock option (ESO)**: A benefit that allows employees to buy company stock at a discounted price, often as part of compensation packages.

- **Employment cost index (ECI)**: A measure of the change in labor costs, including wages and benefits, in the U.S. economy.

- **Endowment fund**: A fund that is typically established by a non-profit organization, such as a university, to manage investments and generate income for long-term purposes.

- **Enterprise Value (EV)**: A measure of a company's total value, calculated as market capitalization plus debt, minority interest, and preferred shares, minus cash and cash equivalents. It represents the cost to acquire a business.

- **Enterprise Value Multiple**: A valuation ratio that compares a company's enterprise value (EV) to a key financial metric, such as earnings before interest, taxes, depreciation, and amortization (EBITDA), to assess the company's value relative to its earnings potential.

- **EPS Diluted**: Earnings per share, accounting for all convertible securities.

- **Equity**: The value of ownership in an asset, such as stocks or real estate, after all liabilities are subtracted.

- **Equity capital**: Money raised by a company through the sale of shares to investors in exchange for ownership interest.

- **Equity financing**: Raising capital by issuing new shares to investors, as opposed to borrowing money (debt financing).

- **Equity index**: A stock market index that measures the performance of a specific group of stocks, such as the S&P 500.

- **Equity market**: The market for buying and selling stocks or shares, typically represented by stock exchanges like the NYSE or NASDAQ.

- **Equity security**: A financial instrument that represents ownership in a company, such as common or preferred stock.

- **ESG (Environmental, Social, Governance)**: Criteria assessing a company's impact in sustainability, social practices, and management ethics.

- **Event-driven strategy**: An investment strategy based on expected market movements due to specific events, such as mergers, acquisitions, or bankruptcies.

- **Ex-dividend date**: The date on or after which a stock is traded without the right to receive the most recent dividend payment.

- **Excess return**: The return on an investment above and beyond the risk-free rate or the expected return.

- **Exchange**: A marketplace where securities, commodities, and other financial instruments are bought and sold, such as the New York Stock Exchange (NYSE) or NASDAQ.

- **Exchange rate**: The price of one currency in terms of another, used in the context of international trade and foreign exchange markets.

- **Exchange-traded fund (ETF)**: A type of investment fund that is traded on stock exchanges, much like individual stocks, and typically tracks an index, commodity, or sector.

- **Exclusivity agreement**: An agreement that limits one party to dealing only with the other party, such as a supplier or distributor relationship.

- **Exercise**: The act of using an option to buy or sell the underlying asset at the strike price.

- **Exercise price**: The price at which the holder of an option can buy or sell the underlying asset when exercising the option.

- **Exit strategy:** A plan for exiting or selling an investment, typically to lock in profits or minimize losses.

- **Expected return**: The anticipated return on an investment based on its historical performance or projected future outcomes.

- **Expense ratio**: The annual fee that funds or ETFs charge to manage investments, expressed as a percentage of assets under management.

- **Expiration date**: The date on which an option or futures contract expires and must be settled or exercised.

A B C D E F G H I J K L M N O P Q R S T U V W X Y Z

F

- **Face value**: The nominal value of a bond or stock, as stated by the issuer, which is typically repaid to the bondholder at maturity.

- **Fallen angel**: A bond that was initially rated investment grade but has since been downgraded to junk status.

- **Favorable variance**: A difference between actual financial performance and the expected performance, where actual results are better than expected.

- **Federal Reserve**: The central bank of the United States responsible for regulating the banking system, managing monetary policy, and maintaining financial stability.

- **Fiduciary**: A person or institution that is legally obligated to act in the best interest of another party, often in the context of managing investments.

- **Fiduciary duty**: The legal and ethical obligation to act in the best interest of another party, such as a trustee to a beneficiary or a financial advisor to a client.

- **Filing deadline**: The final date by which a company must submit financial reports or tax documents to regulatory authorities.

- **Fill or kill (FOK) order**: An order to buy or sell a security that must be filled immediately and in its entirety or not at all.

- **Financial advisor**: A professional who provides advice on managing money, investments, retirement planning, taxes, and other financial matters.

- **Financial engineering**: The use of mathematical techniques and tools to create financial products, manage risk, or optimize investment strategies.

- **Financial leverage**: The use of borrowed funds (debt) to increase the potential return on investment, which can also amplify losses.

- **Financial statement**: A formal record of a company's financial activities, including balance sheets, income statements, and cash flow statements.

- **Financial sponsor**: A private equity firm, venture capital firm, or other institutional investor that provides funding for investments or acquisitions.

- **Financing**: The process of raising capital for business operations, investments, or acquisitions, either through debt or equity.

- **Financing lease**: A type of lease agreement where the lessee effectively assumes ownership of the leased asset at the end of the lease term.

- **Fintech**: Short for "financial technology," it refers to the use of technology to improve and innovate financial services and products.

- **Firm commitment**: A type of underwriting agreement where the underwriter agrees to buy all of the securities being issued, regardless of whether they are sold to investors.

- **Fiscal year**: A 12-month period used for accounting and financial reporting purposes, which may not align with the calendar year.

- **Fixed asset**: A long-term asset that is not intended to be converted into cash within the next 12 months, such as real estate, machinery, or equipment.

- **Fixed Asset Turnover**: Measures how efficiently a company uses its fixed assets (like property, plant, and equipment) to generate revenue.

- **Fixed income**: Investments that provide a regular income, typically through interest payments, such as bonds, preferred stocks, or annuities.

- **Fixed-rate loan**: A loan where the interest rate remains constant over the life of the loan, regardless of changes in market interest rates.

- **Float**: The total number of shares of a company that are available for trading in the market, excluding shares held by insiders or the company itself.

- **Floating rate**: A loan or bond with an interest rate that adjusts periodically based on changes in a benchmark interest rate, such as LIBOR.

- **Floor trader**: A person who buys and sells stocks or other securities on the floor of a stock exchange, typically working for a brokerage firm.

- **Follow-on offering**: A public offering of shares by a company that has already made an initial public offering (IPO), usually to raise additional capital.

- **Foreign exchange (Forex)**: The market for trading currencies, where participants buy and sell currencies from different countries.

- **Forwards contract**: A customized contract between two parties to buy or sell an asset at a specific price at a future date.

- **Free cash flow (FCF)**: The cash generated by a company's operations after subtracting capital expenditures, used for debt repayment, dividends, or reinvestment.

- **Free Cash Flow to Operating Cash Flow Ratio**: Free cash flow as a percentage of operating cash flow.

- **Free rider**: A person or entity that benefits from the efforts of others without contributing or participating, often discussed in the context of market behavior.

- **Freight charges**: The costs associated with transporting goods, typically paid by the buyer or seller depending on the terms of the agreement.

- **Front-running**: The illegal practice of a broker executing orders for their own account based on information about pending orders from clients.

- **Fund**: A pool of money collected from various investors, typically managed by professionals, to invest in securities such as stocks, bonds, or real estate. Funds can be mutual funds, exchange-traded funds (ETFs), or hedge funds, among others.

- **Fund of funds:** An investment strategy that involves investing in a portfolio of other investment funds rather than directly in securities.

- **Fundamentals:** The underlying financial and economic factors that influence the value of a company or asset, such as revenue, earnings, and market share.

- **Fundamental analysis**: The method of evaluating a company or asset based on its financial statements, performance, and other fundamental factors.

- **Futures contract**: A standardized contract that obligates the buyer to purchase, or the seller to sell, an asset at a predetermined price at a future date.

- **Futures market**: A marketplace where futures contracts are traded, often for commodities, financial instruments, or indices.

G

- **Gamma**: Measures the rate of change in delta relative to the underlying asset's price; used in options trading.

- **Gearing**: Ratio of a company's debt relative to its equity; indicates financial leverage.

- **General Obligation Bond**: A municipal bond backed by the credit and taxing power of the issuer.

- **Global Depositary Receipt (GDR)**: A certificate representing shares in foreign companies, traded on international stock exchanges.

- **Golden Parachute**: Large financial benefits for executives if the company is taken over.

- **Good 'Til Canceled (GTC) Order**: An order to buy or sell a stock that remains active until the investor cancels it.

- **Goodwill**: Premium paid over the fair value of a company's net assets during acquisition.

- **Green Bond**: A bond issued to fund projects with positive environmental or climate benefits.

- **Gross Domestic Product (GDP)**: Total value of goods and services produced in a country; used to gauge economic health.

A B C D E F G H I J K L M N O P Q R S T U V W X Y Z

- **Gross Profit**: Revenue minus cost of goods sold.

- **Gross Profit Margin**: Percentage of revenue left after subtracting the cost of goods sold.

- **Growth Stock**: A stock expected to grow at an above-average rate compared to other stocks.

- **Guaranteed Bond**: Bond backed by a company and an additional guarantor for repayment assurance.

- **Guarantor**: A person or entity that promises to cover a borrower's debt in case of default.

H

- **Hard Currency:** A currency that is widely accepted for trade and investment, known for its stability.

- **Hedge:** Strategy to offset potential losses by taking an opposite position in a related asset.

- **Hedge Fund:** An investment fund that employs a wide range of strategies to earn high returns for its investors, including using leverage, short-selling, and derivatives.

- **Hedging Ratio:** The proportion of a position that is covered by a hedge.

- **High-Water Mark:** The highest value reached by an investment or fund before it declines, often used in performance fees for hedge funds.

- **High Yield:** Refers to investments that offer higher returns but come with higher risk, such as junk bonds.

- **Holding Period:** The length of time an investor holds an asset before selling.

- **Horizontal Integration:** Acquiring or merging with competitors in the same industry.

- **Hot Issue:** Newly issued stocks that are in high demand.

- **House Account:** A trading account held by a brokerage firm for itself, not clients.

- **House Margin:** The amount of margin a brokerage firm requires from its own funds.

- **Hull-White Model**: A mathematical model used to price interest rate derivatives.

- **Hybrid Security:** Financial instrument with features of both equity and debt, like convertible bonds.

- **Hypothecation:** The pledging of assets as collateral for a loan without giving up possession of the assets.

I

- **Illiquid Asset**: An asset that cannot be easily sold or converted into cash without a substantial price concession.

- **Income Statement**: A financial report showing a company's revenues, expenses, and profits over a specific period.

- **Income Yield**: The annual income from an investment, expressed as a percentage of its current market price.

- **Implied Volatility**: The estimated volatility of an asset's price, implied by the market price of its options.

- **Index Fund**: A mutual fund or ETF that aims to replicate the performance of a specific market index.

- **Inflation**: The rate at which the general level of prices for goods and services rises, eroding purchasing power.

- **Initial Margin**: The minimum amount of equity required to open a position in margin trading.

- **Initial Public Offering (IPO)**: The first sale of a company's stock to the public, marking its transition to being a publicly traded company.

A B C D E F G H I J K L M N O P Q R S T U V W X Y Z

- **In-the-Money**: A term used for options when they have intrinsic value, meaning the strike price is favorable compared to the market price.

- **Independent Auditor**: A third-party professional who reviews a company's financial statements for accuracy and compliance.

- **Individual Retirement Account (IRA)**: A tax-advantaged retirement account in the United States, available in traditional and Roth formats.

- **Inflation-Linked Bond**: A bond that is indexed to inflation, typically offering returns that adjust with the Consumer Price Index (CPI).

- **Insider Trading**: The illegal practice of trading a company's stock based on non-public, material information.

- **Insolvency**: The state of being unable to meet debt obligations due to insufficient assets.

- **Intangible Assets**: Non-physical assets like patents or trademarks.

- **Interest Coverage**: EBIT divided by interest expenses, showing ability to pay interest.

- **Interest Coverage Ratio**: A measure of a company's ability to meet its interest payments on outstanding debt.

- **Interest Rate**: The cost of borrowing money, usually expressed as a percentage of the principal amount.

- **Intrinsic Value**: The perceived or calculated value of an asset, independent of its market value, based on fundamental analysis.

- **Inventory Turnover**: Indicates how often a company sells and replaces inventory during a period. Higher turnover suggests efficient inventory management.

- **Inverse ETF**: A type of ETF that aims to return the opposite performance of a specific index or asset.

- **Investment Grade**: A rating that indicates a bond or debt instrument is considered low risk by rating agencies.

- **Investment Portfolio**: A collection of financial assets, such as stocks, bonds, and real estate, held by an individual or institution.

- **Issuance**: The process of offering new securities to the market, typically involving stocks or bonds.

J

- **J-Curve**: A theory predicting that a country's trade deficit will worsen before it improves after a currency devaluation.

- **Jacket**: In IPOs, a prospectus cover detailing terms, conditions, and issuer information.

- **Jensen's Alpha**: A performance measure comparing a portfolio's returns to an expected benchmark return.

- **Jobber**: A trader or middleman who buys and sells securities on the market floor, typically in bulk.

- **Jumbo Loan**: A mortgage loan that exceeds conventional loan limits set by regulators.

- **Joint Account**: A brokerage or bank account shared by two or more people with equal rights to the assets.

- **Junior Debt**: Debt that is prioritized lower than other debts in case of default or liquidation.

- **Junk Bond**: A high-yield bond with a lower credit rating, indicating higher risk.

- **January Effect**: A theory suggesting that stocks, particularly small caps, tend to rise in January following year-end tax-loss selling.

- **Jobless Claims**: Weekly statistics on the number of individuals applying for unemployment benefits, indicating labor market strength.

- **Judicial Foreclosure**: A foreclosure process conducted through the court system to settle outstanding mortgage debts.

K

- **Key Performance Indicators (KPIs)**: Metrics used to assess the performance of a company, project, or process in meeting strategic goals.

- **Key Rate Duration**: A measure of the sensitivity of a bond or bond portfolio's value to changes in specific key interest rates, often used in risk management.

- **Keynesian Economics**: An economic theory advocating for government intervention to manage demand and economic cycles, especially during recessions.

- **Kicker**: An additional feature that makes a bond or stock more attractive, such as a warrant attached to a bond.

- **Kill Order**: A directive to cancel an order if it cannot be immediately executed, often used in high-frequency trading.

- **Knock-In Option**: A type of barrier option that becomes active only if the underlying asset's price reaches a specified level.

- **Knock-Out Option**: A barrier option that expires worthless if the underlying asset's price hits a predetermined level.

A
B
C
D
E
F
G
H
I
J
K
L
M
N
O
P
Q
R
S
T
U
V
W
X
Y
Z

L

- **Lagging Indicator**: An economic factor that shows a delayed reaction to market trends, like unemployment rates.

- **Large-Cap Stock**: Shares of a company with a high market capitalization, typically over $10 billion.

- **Last Sale Price**: The most recent transaction price for a security.

- **LBO (Leveraged Buyout)**: Purchase of a company using borrowed funds, often using the company's assets as collateral.

- **Leading Indicator**: Economic factors predicting future market trends, such as new orders or stock prices.

- **Leverage**: Use of borrowed funds to amplify investment returns.

- **Leveraged ETF**: An exchange-traded fund that uses debt to enhance returns, often 2x or 3x the index movement.

- **Leverage Ratio**: A measure of a company's debt level relative to equity or assets, used to assess financial risk.

- **Liabilities**: Debts or obligations a company must settle in the future.

- **Limit Order**: Instruction to buy or sell a stock at a specified price or better.

- **Limit Up/Limit Down**: The maximum and minimum price movement allowed in a trading day for a stock or commodity.

- **Liquidity**: The ease with which an asset can be quickly converted into cash without affecting its price.

- **Listed Security**: Stock that is traded on a registered exchange like the NYSE.

- **Load**: Fee charged when purchasing (front-end load) or selling (back-end load) a mutual fund.

- **Long Position**: Holding a security with the expectation its value will rise. The opposite of a short position.

- **Long-Term Capital Gain**: Profit on an asset held longer than one year, often taxed at a lower rate.

- **Long-Term Debt to Capitalization**: Long-term debt as a percentage of total capital.

- **Lot**: The standard trading quantity, such as 100 shares, referred to as a "round lot."

- **Low**: The lowest trading price of a security within a given period.

- **Loss Aversion**: An investor's tendency to prefer avoiding losses over acquiring equivalent gains, often influencing trading behavior.

- **Low Beta Stock**: A stock with a beta less than 1, indicating lower volatility compared to the overall market.

- **Low P/E Stocks**: Stocks with a low price-to-earnings ratio, potentially undervalued.

- **Lump-Sum Payment**: Single large payment, often for investment or debt settlement.

- **Liquidity Ratio**: Measure of a company's ability to cover short-term liabilities with liquid assets.

A B C D E F G H I J K L M N O P Q R S T U V W X Y Z

M

- **MACD (Moving Average Convergence Divergence)**: A trend-following indicator showing the relationship between two moving averages of a stock's price.

- **Maintenance Margin**: The minimum account balance an investor must maintain before a broker will demand additional funds.

- **Majority Shareholder**: An individual or entity that owns more than 50% of a company's shares, holding significant control.

- **Managed Fund**: An investment fund actively managed by a professional to meet specific goals, such as growth or income.

- **Margin Account**: A brokerage account allowing investors to borrow funds to buy securities, using the securities as collateral.

- **Margin Call**: A demand by a broker for an investor to deposit more funds or sell assets to cover potential losses.

- **Market Breadth**: A technical analysis indicator measuring the number of stocks advancing versus declining in a given market.

- **Market Capitalization**: The total market value of a company's outstanding shares, calculated as share price times shares outstanding.

- **Market Correction**: A decline of 10% or more in the price of a stock index or individual asset, typically occurring after rapid gains.

- **Market Index**: A measurement of a section of the stock market, often used to describe the performance of a specific group of stocks (e.g., S&P 500).

- **Market Maker**: A firm or individual providing liquidity by buying and selling a particular stock on demand.

- **Market Order**: An order to buy or sell a security immediately at the current market price.

- **Market Price**: The current price at which a stock or other security can be bought or sold.

- **Market Risk**: The potential financial loss due to movements in market prices or volatility.

- **Market Sentiment**: The overall attitude of investors toward a particular security or the financial markets in general.

- **Market Surveillance**: The monitoring of trading activity to detect and prevent abusive practices like insider trading or market manipulation.

- **Market Timing**: The strategy of making buy or sell decisions based on predictions of future market price movements.

- **Market Value**: The price at which an asset would trade in a competitive auction setting.

- **Mean Reversion**: A theory suggesting that asset prices and returns eventually return to long-term average levels.

- **Micro Cap**: Companies with very small market capitalizations, typically less than $300 million, often highly volatile.

- **Mid Cap**: Companies with medium-sized market capitalizations, generally between $2 billion and $10 billion.

- **Minority Interest**: Share of subsidiary earnings not owned by the parent company.

- **Momentum Investing**: An investment strategy focused on buying stocks with rising prices and selling those with falling prices.

- **Money Market Fund**: A mutual fund that invests in short-term, high-quality debt securities, known for stability and liquidity.

A
B
C
D
E
F
G
H
I
J
K
L
M
N
O
P
Q
R
S
T
U
V
W
X
Y
Z

- **Mortgage**: A loan used to purchase property, where the property itself serves as collateral for the loan. The borrower repays the loan in installments over time.

- **Mortgage-Backed Securities (MBS)**: Investment products backed by a pool of home loans, where the payments made by homeowners are passed on to investors.

- **Moving Average**: A commonly used indicator that smooths price data to identify trends by averaging past prices over a specified period.

- **Multi-Cap Fund**: A mutual fund that invests across small, mid, and large-cap companies, offering diversified exposure.

- **Mutual Fund**: A type of investment vehicle made up of a pool of money collected from many investors to invest in securities like stocks, bonds, and other assets.

A B C D E F G H I J K L **M** N O P Q R S T U V W X Y Z

N

- **Naked Call**: An options trading strategy where the seller does not own the underlying asset but sells the right to buy it at a specific price.

- **Naked Put**: An options strategy where the seller does not own the underlying asset and sells the right to sell it at a specific price.

- **Narrow Market**: A market where only a few stocks or sectors are actively trading, limiting investment opportunities.

- **NASDAQ**: A global electronic marketplace for buying and selling securities, known for its technology-focused listings.

- **Nasdaq-100**: An index that includes the 100 largest non-financial companies listed on the NASDAQ stock exchange.

- **Negative Equity**: When a company's liabilities exceed its assets, leading to a deficit on the balance sheet.

- **Net Asset Value (NAV)**: The total value of a mutual fund's assets minus its liabilities, often used to determine the price of a share in a fund.

- **Net Income**: The total profit of a company after all expenses, taxes, and costs have been deducted from total revenue.

- **Net Income per EBT**: Ratio of net income to earnings before taxes, showing after-tax profitability.

- **Net Margin**: A profitability ratio calculated by dividing net income by total revenue, showing the percentage of profit generated from sales.

- **Net Return**: The return on an investment after all costs, fees, and taxes have been deducted.

- **Neutral Position**: A position in options trading where an investor holds equal amounts of calls and puts, aiming to benefit from minimal movement in the underlying asset.

- **New Issue**: The initial sale of stock or bonds, usually by a company going public or issuing new debt.

- **New York Stock Exchange (NYSE)**: One of the largest and most well-known stock exchanges in the world, based in New York City.

- **Non-GAAP Earnings**: Earnings calculated without including certain expenses, as opposed to Generally Accepted Accounting Principles (GAAP).

- **Normalized Earnings**: Earnings adjusted for non-recurring events to provide a clearer picture of a company's long-term performance.

- **Nominal Return**: The return on an investment before inflation or taxes are taken into account.

- **No Load Fund**: A mutual fund that does not charge a sales fee or commission when buying or selling shares.

- **Nominal Yield**: The interest rate paid by a bond relative to its face value, without adjusting for inflation or other factors.

- **Non-Convertible Bond**: A bond that cannot be converted into shares of stock in the issuing company.

- **Non-Current Assets**: Long-term assets not expected to be liquidated within a year.

- **Non-Investment Grade**: Refers to bonds rated below investment grade, often considered speculative or high-risk investments.

- **Non-Operating Income**: Income generated from activities outside the core operations of a company, such as investments or asset sales.

- **Normalized Price**: A price adjusted to account for changes in market conditions, inflation, or other external factors.

- **Notional Value**: The total value of a leveraged position in the derivatives market, calculated by multiplying the number of contracts by the price of the underlying asset.

- **Nudge**: A concept from behavioral economics where small changes in the presentation of information influence decisions, such as encouraging savings or investments.

- **Obligor**: The party in a bond agreement responsible for repaying the principal and interest to bondholders.

- **Off-Balance Sheet Financing**: A method of financing that does not appear on a company's balance sheet, often used to keep liabilities hidden from investors.

- **Offer Price**: The price at which a seller is willing to sell a security in the market.

- **Ongoing Capital**: The capital a company requires to continue its operations, often considered as working capital.

- **Open-End Fund**: A type of investment fund that issues new shares or redeems existing shares at the current net asset value (NAV).

- **Open Market Operations**: The buying and selling of government securities by a central bank to regulate the money supply and influence interest rates.

- **Open Position**: A position in a security that has not yet been closed or offset, meaning the investor still holds the asset or contract.

- **Operating Cash Flow**: Cash generated from regular business operations.

- **Operating Cash Flow to Sales Ratio**: Operating cash flow as a percentage of sales, indicating efficiency.

- **Operating Cycle**: The total time it takes for a company to buy inventory, sell products, and collect cash from sales.

- **Operating Income**: The profit a company makes from its regular business operations, excluding income from non-operating activities like investments or asset sales.

- **Operating Profit Margin**: Percentage of revenue left after operating expenses, excluding interest and taxes.

- **Option**: A financial derivative that gives the holder the right, but not the obligation, to buy or sell an underlying asset at a predetermined price within a specific time period.

- **Option Premium**: The price paid for an option, representing the cost of purchasing the right to buy or sell an underlying asset.

- **Order Book**: A record of buy and sell orders for a particular security in a financial market, used to determine the supply and demand for that security.

A B C D E F G H I J K L M N O P Q R S T U V W X Y Z

- **Outstanding Shares**: The total number of shares that have been issued by a company and are currently held by shareholders, excluding treasury shares.

- **Overbought**: A market condition where the price of a security has risen too quickly and may be due for a correction.

- **Oversold**: A market condition where the price of a security has fallen too quickly and may be due for a rebound.

- **Over-the-Counter (OTC)**: A decentralized market where securities are traded directly between parties, without a centralized exchange.

- **Overcapitalization**: A situation where a company has more capital than it can profitably employ, often leading to inefficiencies.

- **Overdraft**: A situation where an account holder withdraws more money from an account than is available, often subject to fees and interest.

P

- **P/E Ratio (Price-to-Earnings Ratio)**: A valuation ratio calculated by dividing the current share price by the earnings per share (EPS) of the company, used to assess whether a stock is overvalued or undervalued.

- **PEG Ratio**: Price-to-earnings ratio adjusted for expected earnings growth.

- **Passive Investing**: A strategy of investing in a market index or a broad portfolio of assets, with little to no active management.

- **Payables Turnover**: Reflects how quickly a company pays its suppliers. A higher ratio suggests faster payments.

- **Payout Ratio**: The proportion of a company's earnings paid out to shareholders in the form of dividends, often used to assess the sustainability of the dividend.

- **Penny Stock**: A stock that trades for less than $5 per share, often associated with small, speculative companies.

- **Performance Fee**: A fee charged by an investment manager based on the return generated by the fund, often in hedge funds or private equity.

A B C D E F G H I J K L M N O P Q R S T U V W X Y Z

- **Portfolio**: A collection of financial assets such as stocks, bonds, and cash equivalents held by an individual or institution.

- **Point**: A unit of measure used to indicate changes in the price of a security, typically equal to a one-dollar change in price.

- **Premium**: The amount by which a bond's market price exceeds its face value or the amount paid for an option contract.

- **Pretax Profit Margin**: Profit as a percentage of revenue before taxes are deducted.

- **Price Action**: The movement of a security's price over time, often used by traders to analyze market trends and make decisions.

- **Price-to-Book (P/B) Ratio**: A financial ratio comparing a company's market value to its book value, used to assess whether a stock is undervalued or overvalued.

- **Price to Cash Flow (P/CF) Ratio**: A valuation ratio comparing a company's market price to its cash flow per share, showing how much investors are willing to pay for each dollar of cash generated.

- **Price Earnings to Growth (PEG) Ratio**: A valuation metric that compares a company's price-to-earnings (P/E) ratio to its earnings growth rate, helping to assess the value of the stock in relation to its expected future growth.

- **Price-to-Free Cash Flow (P/FCF)**: A ratio comparing a company's market price to its free cash flow, showing how much investors pay for each dollar of free cash flow.

- **Price to Operating Cash Flow (P/OCF) Ratio:** A ratio comparing a company's market price to its operating cash flow, indicating how much investors pay for each dollar of cash generated by operations.

- **Price-to-Sales (P/S) Ratio**: A valuation ratio comparing a company's stock price to its revenues per share, often used to evaluate the stock of companies with no earnings.

- **Private Equity**: Investments made in private companies or buyouts of public companies, typically involving a group of investors or firms.

- **Privatization**: The process of converting a public company into a private one by buying back its publicly traded shares.

- **Proceeds**: The money raised from the sale of securities or assets.

- **Put Option**: A financial contract that gives the holder the right, but not the obligation, to sell an underlying asset at a predetermined price within a specific time frame.

- **Put-Call Parity**: A financial principle that defines the relationship between the prices of European call and put options with the same strike price and expiration date.

- **Pledge**: To offer securities as collateral for a loan or debt obligation.

- **Primary Dealer**: A financial institution authorized to deal directly with a country's central bank in the buying and selling of government securities.

- **Pre-market Trading**: The trading that occurs before the official market open, typically from 4:00 AM to 9:30 AM EST in the U.S.

- **Post-market Trading**: The trading that occurs after the official market close, typically from 4:00 PM to 8:00 PM EST in the U.S.

- **Price Movement**: The change in the price of a security over a given period, indicating the strength of a trend.

- **Q Ratio (Tobin's Q)**: A ratio comparing a company's market value to the replacement cost of its assets. A high Q ratio suggests that a company is overvalued.

- **Qualitative Analysis**: A method of evaluating investments by examining non-quantifiable factors, such as management quality, industry cycles, and company culture.

- **Quantitative Analysis**: The use of mathematical models and statistical techniques to analyze financial data and make investment decisions.

- **Quant Fund**: A type of investment fund that uses quantitative analysis to make trading decisions, often relying on algorithms and complex models.

- **Quarter**: A three-month period in a company's financial calendar, used for reporting earnings and other financial data.

- **Quarterly Earnings Report**: A report released every quarter by publicly traded companies that includes financial performance, such as revenue, net income, and earnings per share.

- **Quick Ratio (Acid-Test Ratio)**: A measure of a company's short-term liquidity, calculated by dividing liquid assets (cash, marketable securities, and receivables) by current liabilities.

- **Quiet Period**: A time frame during which a company that has filed for an IPO or is releasing earnings is restricted from making public statements that could affect its stock price.

- **Quota**: A fixed number of securities, goods, or services a company or organization is allowed to produce, sell, or import within a certain period.

- **Quantitative Easing (QE)**: A monetary policy in which a central bank purchases government bonds or other financial assets to increase money supply and stimulate the economy.

- **Qualified Dividend**: A type of dividend taxed at the capital gains rate rather than ordinary income rate if certain criteria are met.

- **Qualifying Round**: The preliminary stage of a competitive bidding process, often required for investments in certain markets or assets.

- **Quasi-Public Corporation**: A company that operates as a private corporation but has some government oversight or involvement.

A B C D E F G H I J K L M N O P Q R S T U V W X Y Z

R

- **Rally**: A period during which the price of a stock, market index, or asset experiences a sustained upward trend.

- **Rate of Return (ROR)**: The percentage of profit or loss made on an investment relative to its cost.

- **Ratings Agency**: An organization that evaluates and assigns credit ratings to companies and governments based on their financial stability and ability to repay debt.

- **R&D Expense**: Cost of research and development activities.

- **Real Estate Investment Trust (REIT)**: A company that owns, operates, or finances income-generating real estate, allowing investors to earn income from property without direct ownership.

- **Rebalancing**: The process of adjusting the weightings of assets in a portfolio to maintain a desired allocation.

- **Receivables**: Amount owed to the company by customers.

- **Receivables Turnover**: Measures how quickly a company collects its receivables. A higher ratio indicates better collection efficiency.

- **Record Date**: The date by which an investor must be listed as a shareholder to receive dividends or participate in corporate actions.

- **Redemption**: The repayment of a fixed-income security, such as a bond, at or before its maturity date.

- **Relative Strength Index (RSI)**: A momentum indicator that measures the speed and change of price movements, typically used to identify overbought or oversold conditions.

- **Residual Income**: The net income that an investment generates beyond the minimum required return.

- **Resistance Level**: A price point at which a stock or market tends to face selling pressure, preventing further upward movement. It's often used by traders to identify potential reversal points.

- **Retained Earnings**: The portion of a company's profits not paid out as dividends but reinvested in the business or used to pay off debt.

- **Return on Assets (ROA)**: A measure of how effectively a company uses its assets to generate profit, calculated as net income divided by total assets.

- **Return on Capital Employed (ROCE)**: Efficiency of capital use to generate operating profit.

- **Return on Equity (ROE)**: A measure of a company's profitability, calculated by dividing net income by shareholders' equity.

- **Revenue**: The total income generated by a company from its business activities, such as sales of goods or services.

- **Reverse Stock Split**: A corporate action that reduces the number of a company's outstanding shares and increases the share price proportionately.

- **Rights Issue**: An offer made by a company to its existing shareholders to buy additional shares at a discounted price.

- **Risk-Adjusted Return**: A measure of an investment's return that takes into account the level of risk involved.

- **Roadshow**: A series of presentations by a company's management team to potential investors, often preceding an IPO.

- **Roth IRA**: A type of individual retirement account in the U.S. where contributions are made with after-tax dollars, and withdrawals are tax-free in retirement.

- **Run Rate**: The projected financial performance of a company based on current results, often annualized to estimate future revenue or profit.

- **Russell 2000 Index**: A benchmark index of 2,000 small-cap U.S. stocks, widely used to measure the performance of smaller companies.

S

- **S&P 500 (Standard & Poor's 500)**: A stock market index tracking 500 large-cap U.S. companies.

- **Safe Haven**: Investments like gold or bonds that are expected to retain value during market downturns.

- **Scalping**: A trading strategy focused on making small profits from rapid trades throughout the day.

- **Secondary Market**: The market where investors buy and sell securities from each other rather than from the issuing company.

- **Sector**: A broad grouping of industries within the stock market, such as technology, healthcare, or energy.

- **Securities**: Financial instruments that represent ownership (stocks) or debt (bonds) and can be traded.

- **Securities and Exchange Commission (SEC)**: The U.S. federal agency responsible for enforcing securities laws and regulating the stock market.

- **Security Token**: A digital token that represents ownership of an asset, regulated like traditional securities.

A B C D E F G H I J K L M N O P Q R S T U V W X Y Z

- **Sell-Off**: A rapid selling of securities, leading to a decline in stock prices.

- **SG&A Expenses**: Selling, general, and administrative costs.

- **Settlement Date**: The date on which a stock trade is finalized, typically two business days after the trade date (T+2).

- **Share Buyback**: When a company repurchases its own shares, reducing the number of shares outstanding and often increasing share value.

- **Share Price**: The price of a single share of a company's stock.

- **Shareholder Equity**: The residual interest in a company's assets after deducting liabilities, representing owners' claims.

- **Short Interest**: The total number of shares of a stock that have been sold short but not yet covered.

- **Short Selling**: Borrowing and selling a stock in anticipation of buying it back later at a lower price to profit from a price drop.

- **Short-Term Coverage Ratio**: Measures ability to cover short-term liabilities with short-term assets.

- **Short-Term Gain**: Profit from selling an asset held for one year or less, typically taxed at a higher rate than long-term gains.

- **Small Cap**: Companies with a relatively small market capitalization, typically between $300 million and $2 billion.

- **Slippage**: The difference between the expected price of a trade and the actual price at which it is executed.

- **Sovereign Bond**: A bond issued by a national government to raise funds, often considered low-risk.

- **Speculation**: Investing in assets with a high degree of risk in the hope of significant returns.

- **Special Purpose Acquisition Company (SPAC)**: A company formed to raise capital through an IPO with the intention of acquiring an existing company.

- **Spot Price**: The current market price at which an asset is bought or sold for immediate delivery.

- **Spread**: The difference between the bid price (what buyers are willing to pay) and the ask price (what sellers want).

- **Spread Betting**: A speculative strategy where investors bet on the price movement of a stock without owning it.

- **Stock Dividend**: A dividend payment made in the form of additional shares rather than cash.

- **Stock Exchange**: A marketplace for buying and selling stocks, such as the NYSE or NASDAQ.

- **Stock Market Bubble**: A market condition where stock prices are inflated far beyond their intrinsic value.

- **Stock Market Crash**: A sudden and significant decline in stock prices across major markets.

- **Stock Option**: A financial derivative giving the holder the right, but not the obligation, to buy or sell stock at a specific price.

- **Stock Portfolio**: A collection of stocks owned by an individual or institution.

- **Stock Split**: When a company increases the number of its outstanding shares to make the stock more affordable without changing the company's market capitalization.

- **Stop Limit Order**: An order to buy or sell a stock at a specified price or better, activated once a certain price is reached.

A
B
C
D
E
F
G
H
I
J
K
L
M
N
O
P
Q
R
S
T
U
V
W
X
Y
Z

- **Stop Order (Stop-Loss)**: An order to buy or sell a stock once it reaches a specific price, used to limit losses or lock in profits.

- **Straddle**: An options strategy involving buying or selling both a call and a put with the same strike price.

- **Strangle**: An options strategy where the investor holds a call and a put with different strike prices.

- **Strike Price**: The price at which an options contract can be exercised.

- **Subscription Rights**: Rights offered to existing shareholders to purchase additional shares, often at a discount.

- **Support Level**: A price level where a stock tends to find buying interest, preventing further price decline. The opposite of a resistance.

- **Swing Trading**: A trading strategy where traders seek to capture short- to medium-term gains in a stock over several days or weeks.

- **Systematic Risk**: The risk inherent to the entire market or a market segment, which cannot be diversified away.

T

- **Takeover**: Acquisition of one company by another, often by purchasing a majority of its shares.

- **Tangible Asset**: Physical assets like property or equipment that have value.

- **Target Date Fund**: A fund designed for a specific investment goal or retirement date.

- **Target Price**: The price level analysts expect a security to reach in a specific timeframe.

- **Tax-Advantaged Account**: Investment accounts that offer tax benefits, like IRAs or 401(k)s.

- **Tax-Loss Harvesting**: Selling securities at a loss to offset taxable gains.

- **Technical Analysis**: Evaluating securities by analyzing statistics from trading activity, such as price and volume.

- **Tender Offer**: A public offer to purchase shares from shareholders, usually at a premium to the current price.

- **Thin Market**: A market with low trading volume and limited liquidity.

- **Tick Size**: The minimum price movement of a security.

- **Ticker Symbol**: A unique series of letters representing a publicly traded company's stock, such as *MSFT (Microsoft)* or *NVDA (Nvidia)*.

- **Time Value**: The portion of an option's price based on time remaining until expiration.

- **Top-Down Analysis**: A macroeconomic approach to investing, starting with sectors and moving to individual companies.

- **Total Debt to Capitalization**: Total debt as a percentage of total capital.

- **Total Return**: The combined return of dividends, interest, and capital appreciation over a specific period.

- **Tracking Error**: The difference between a portfolio's returns and its benchmark's returns.

- **Trailing Stop Order**: A stop order that adjusts as the stock price moves, aiming to lock in profits.

- **TTM (Trailing Twelve Months)**: Refers to financial metrics measured over the past 12 months.

- **Transaction Costs**: Fees associated with buying or selling securities, such as commissions and spreads.

A B C D E F G H I J K L M N O P Q R S T U V W X Y Z

- **Treasury Bond (T-Bond)**: A long-term debt security issued by the U.S. government with maturities of over 10 years.

- **Treasury Inflation-Protected Securities (TIPS)**: Government bonds indexed to inflation.

- **Treasury Stock**: Shares that a company has repurchased and holds in its treasury.

- **Trendline**: A line drawn on a chart to identify the direction of a trend.

- **Triple Bottom**: A bullish technical pattern indicating a reversal after three similar lows.

- **Triple Witching**: The simultaneous expiration of stock options, stock index futures, and stock index options.

- **Turnover Ratio**: A measure of a portfolio's trading activity over a specific period.

- **Two-Way Quote**: A price quote that shows both the bid (buy) and ask (sell) price for a security.

- **Type A Fund**: A fund structured to grow over time by reinvesting its income.

U

- **UCITS**: Undertakings for Collective Investment in Transferable Securities. European Union standards for transparency and investor protection.

- **Underperformance**: When an asset or investment performs worse than a relevant benchmark or market index.

- **Underwriter**: A financial institution or individual that assesses and takes on the risk of issuing securities for a company or government.

- **Undervalued**: A term used to describe a security that is trading for less than its intrinsic value.

- **Unsecured Debt**: Debt that is not backed by collateral and relies on the borrower's creditworthiness.

- **Unit Trust**: A pooled investment fund where investors' money is managed collectively and divided into units, typically used in the UK.

- **Uptrend**: A market condition where the prices of assets are consistently rising over time.

- **Uptick**: A price movement where a stock's price increases compared to its last transaction price.

- **Usury**: The illegal practice of lending money at excessively high-interest rates.

- **Utility Stocks**: Stocks from companies that provide essential services like water, electricity, and gas, often seen as stable investments.

- <u>**U.S. Treasury Bonds**</u>: Debt securities issued by the U.S. government, considered low-risk investments.

- **Unrealized Gain**: The profit on an investment that has not been sold yet.

- **Unrealized Loss**: A loss on an investment that has not yet been sold or realized.

- **Upward Mobility**: The potential for an asset or investment to increase in value over time.

- **Uptick Rule**: A regulation that only allows short sales to be executed at a higher price than the last transaction price.

V

- **Valuation**: The process of determining the current worth of an asset or company.

- **Value Investing**: A strategy of buying undervalued stocks based on financial analysis, aiming for long-term gains.

- **Value Stock**: A stock that is considered undervalued compared to its fundamentals, such as earnings or dividends.

- **Value-at-Risk (VaR)**: A risk management tool used to estimate the potential loss in value of a portfolio over a defined period for a given confidence interval.

- **Venture Capital**: Funds provided to startups and small businesses with high growth potential in exchange for equity or an ownership stake.

- **Vertical Merger**: A merger between two companies operating in the same industry but at different stages of the production process.

- **Volatility**: A statistical measure of the dispersion of returns for a given security or market index, often used as an indicator of risk.

- **Volatility Index (VIX)**: A measure of market expectation of near-term volatility, often referred to as the "fear gauge."

- **Volume**: The number of shares or contracts traded in a security or market during a given period of time, indicating the activity level and liquidity of the asset.

- **Vulture Capital**: Investment made in distressed companies, typically with the goal of turning around their financial position or selling assets for profit.

- **Variable Rate**: A type of interest rate that changes over time based on market conditions.

- **Volatility Smile**: A pattern in options pricing where implied volatility is higher for both low and high strike prices compared to the middle range.

- **Volatility Risk Premium**: The difference between the expected volatility of an asset or market and the actual volatility.

- **VIX Futures**: Futures contracts that track the Volatility Index, used to trade or hedge market volatility.

A B C D E F G H I J K L M N O P Q R S T U V W X Y Z

- **Wagering**: The act of making bets on the performance of a financial asset, typically seen in speculative markets.

- **Wash Sale**: A sale of a security at a loss, followed by purchasing the same or similar security within 30 days, disallowing the loss for tax purposes.

- **Weighted Average Cost of Capital (WACC)**: The average rate of return a company must pay to finance its operations with both debt and equity.

- **Weighted Average Shares**: Average number of shares outstanding during a reporting period.

- **Weighted Average Shares Diluted Growth**: Change in diluted shares over time.

- **Weighted Index**: An index where individual components are weighted according to their market value or other factors.

- **Whale**: A term for an investor or institution with a large amount of capital to invest, able to move markets with their trades.

- **Whipsaw**: A market condition in which prices move sharply in one direction, then quickly reverse.

- **Windfall**: An unexpected gain, usually from a one-time event like the sale of assets or favorable changes in the market.

- **Warrant**: A security that gives the holder the right to purchase stock at a specific price within a certain timeframe.

- **Working Capital**: The difference between a company's current assets and current liabilities, indicating its operational liquidity.

- **World Bank**: An international financial institution that provides loans to countries for development projects, impacting global markets.

- **World Stock Index**: A stock market index that includes global stocks, used to measure global market performance.

- **Write-off**: The reduction of the value of an asset or a debt that is unlikely to be recovered.

- **X-Date**: The date on which a dividend is declared and the price of a stock is reduced by the amount of the dividend.

- **X-Index**: A stock market index that tracks a specific segment or factor, such as a sector or size of companies.

- **X-Rate**: The exchange rate between two currencies.

A B C D E F G H I J K L M N O P Q R S T U V W X Y Z

Y

- **Yankee Bond**: A bond issued by a foreign entity in the U.S. market, denominated in U.S. dollars.

- **Yellow Flag**: A warning signal in trading that alerts traders to watch for potential issues with an investment.

- **Yen Carry Trade**: A strategy where investors borrow yen (Japanese currency) at low interest rates to invest in higher-yielding assets in other currencies.

- **Yield**: The income return on an investment, expressed as a percentage of the investment's cost or market value.

- **Yield Curve**: A graph that shows the relationship between interest rates and the maturity of debt for a given borrower in the bond market.

- **Yield Spread**: The difference in yields between two different debt securities, often used to compare bonds of different credit ratings or maturities.

- **Yield to Maturity (YTM)**: The total return an investor can expect to earn if a bond is held until it matures.

- **<u>YTD (Year-to-Date)</u>**: The period from the beginning of the current calendar year up to the present date.

- **YoY (Year-over-Year)**: A comparison of a company's financial performance for a specific period with the same period in the previous year.

Z

- **Zero-Coupon Bond**: A bond that doesn't pay periodic interest but is sold at a deep discount and matures at face value.

- **Z-Score**: A statistical measurement used to predict the likelihood of a company going bankrupt, often used in financial analysis.

- **Zombie Company**: A company that is only able to meet its debt obligations through new borrowing, often struggling or unprofitable.

- **Zero-Interest Loan**: A loan where no interest is charged on the principal during the life of the loan, typically used for promotional financing.

- **Zero-Liquidation Risk**: A situation where a company is unlikely to have its assets liquidated, as it is sufficiently solvent or profitable.

www.ingramcontent.com/pod-product-compliance
Lightning Source LLC
Chambersburg PA
CBHW032211220526
45472CB00018B/1074